I am with you always

Words of comfort in times of illness

To

....

From

....

Jarrold Colour Publications, Norwich.

Fallow deer pause in the dappled sunshine

Acknowledgements

Scripture quotations used by kind permission: From Hosea, Job, Romans and Matthew, *Good News Bible* 1976, the Bible Societies and Collins, © American Bible Society; from *The Psalms: A New Translation for Worship*, © English Text 1976, 1977, David L Frost, John A Emerton, Andrew A Macintosh, © Wm Collins Sons & Co Ltd; from Deuteronomy and Ecclesiastes, *New English Bible* © 1970 Oxford & Cambridge University Presses.

Other quotations taken from *Gospel Meditations*, Louis Evely, Mowbrays; *Approaching Easter*, Joyce Huggett, Lion Publishing plc; *Assemblies for School Children's Church*, R H Lloyd, Religious & Moral Education Press; *A Far-off Place*, Laurens van der Post, Hogarth Press; *Stories & Prayers at Five to Ten*, Richard Tatlock, Mowbrays; the hymn 'Lord of all hopefulness, (1 verse omitted) by Jan Struther from *Enlarged Songs of Praise*, © Oxford University Press. Every effort has been made to trace and acknowledge ownership of copyright; however, copyright has in some cases proved untraceable.

From the depths

Longing

As pants the hart for cooling streams
When heated in the chase,
So longs my soul, O God, for thee,
And thy refreshing grace.

For thee, my God, the living God,
My thirsty soul doth pine:
O when shall I behold thy face,
Thou majesty divine?

N Tate and N Brady

Sheepwash Bridge, Ashford, near Bakewell, Derbyshire

Please, God

A man named Lazarus, who lived in Bethany, was ill. His sisters, Martha and Mary, knew Jesus well. They sent a message to Jesus:

'Lord, the one you love is sick.'

John 11:3

This is the simplest prayer in illness or any kind of need. You can say it for yourself or for someone else.

If you are able to, it might help you to picture Jesus caring for Peter's mother-in-law, or one of the leprosy sufferers, or the paralysed man whose friends carried him to the crowded house. He always understood the need and the pain.

'Lord, the one you love is sick.' No other words are needed.

Looking across Loch Lomond from Luss

The tranquil beauty of an English lakeside scene

Church and cottages at Clavering, Essex

God-forsaken?

O Lord, hear my prayer
  and let my cry come to you.
Do not hide your face from me in the day of my trouble
  turn your ear to me;
and when I call, be swift to answer.
For my days pass away like smoke,
and my bones burn as in a furnace.
My heart is scorched and withered like grass,
and I forget to eat my bread.

The psalmist poured out his pain and misery in these words.
And it may be that by expressing his feelings in this way he
found relief. For he goes on in more hopeful mood:

'But you, Lord, are enthroned for ever,
and your name shall be known throughout all generations.
You will arise and have mercy. . .'

Psalm 102: 1–4, 12

Blakeney, Norfolk

Pain

Your pain is the breaking of the shell that encloses your
understanding. Even as the stone of the fruit must break,
that its heart may stand in the sun, so must you know pain.

Kahlil Gibran, The Prophet

Pain may be a necessary part of life, but that doesn't stop it
hurting!

When life hurts, we need not 'go it alone'. We can ask for
God's help to keep us from falling. And He will not let us down.

How can I give you up?
How can I abandon you?
My heart will not let me do it!
My love for you is too strong.

Hosea 11:8

Cheltenham, Gloucestershire

The splendour of Wells Cathedral

Weariness

Hold Thou my hands!
In grief and joy, in hope and fear
Lord, let me feel that thou art near,
Hold Thou my hands!

W. Canton

Though he stumble, he shall not fall;
for the Lord grasps him by the hand.

Psalm 37:24

The dramatic Bude coastline at Millook, Cornwall

The Five Sisters of Kintail look down over Loch Duich

Statue of Sir Winston Churchill at Westerham, Kent

Black Dog

Winston Churchill, whose name conjures up Victory, was constantly fighting a battle within himself: he had recurring fits of depression, which he nicknamed Black Dog. Throughout his life he had to choose between saying, 'Down, boy' or being defeated by this attacking creature. He cultivated that certain kind of moral courage that would not give in, and became the strong leader who inspired the British and their Allies in dangerous times.

> *Be strong, be resolute; you must not dread them or be afraid, for the Lord your God himself goes with you; he will not fail you or forsake you.*
>
> Deuteronomy 31:6

Before the storm, Padstow, Cornwall

Helplessness

Other refuge have I none;
Hangs my helpless soul on thee;
Leave, ah! Leave me not alone,
Still support and comfort me.
All my trust in thee is stayed,
All my help from thee I bring;
Cover my defenceless head
With the shadow of thy wing.

                              Charles Wesley

Howden Reservoir, Derbyshire

Desolation

I will lift up mine eyes unto the hills.
From whence cometh my help?
My help cometh even from the Lord
who hath made heaven and earth.

Psalm 121: 1–2

The psalmist lifted up his eye
For help to sun-scarred crag and sky,
To peaks of arid majesty –
Carmel, Hermon, Sinai –
Bitter, barren, burning slopes
Devoid of joy, bereft of hope,
And there discerned, in rock and heat,
The God his heart so yearned to meet.

Breathtaking Highland scenery near Drumrunie

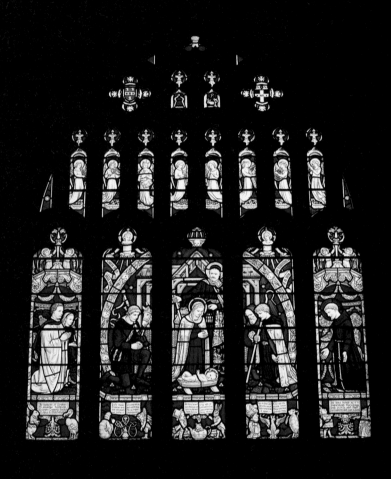

A Wonderland in stained glass – Lewis Carroll's memorial at Daresbury, Cheshire

Transformation
Rejects

Long ago, when the stonemasons had almost finished building one of the great cathedrals, an unknown craftsman appeared and asked to be allowed to do a stained glass window. He wanted no payment, so the master builder gave permission, thinking that if it turned out badly his skilled glaziers could knock it out and start again.

The newcomer was left to his own devices and for months he worked behind a screen till it was finished.

To his amazement, the master builder saw a window of indescribable beauty and asked where such exquisite glass with such glorious colours had come from.

The craftsman replied, 'Sir, I picked it up here and there inside and outside the cathedral. This window is made up of all the fragments that had been thrown away as useless.'

> *There is no waste in love.*
> *Love useth all the little, outworn things,*
> *Dropt leaf, and sea-snail's ruined coracle,*
> *Dead bird with rumpled wings,*
> *To build anew a universe that sings.*
>
> Dulcie Eden Greville

Acceptance

Joni Eareckson is a person who with God's help turned tragedy into triumph. When she was 17 a diving accident resulted in total paralysis of body and limbs, with strength only to move her head. The realisation that her injury was permanent plunged her into suicidal depression. How could she endure the rest of her life as a quadriplegic?

The answer must be, pray for a miracle! Joni and her young Christian friends prayed with all their hearts, but it became more and more clear that she would never so much as drink a glass of water without help. She felt betrayed, bitterly angry with God.

Through terrible bouts of rebellion, doubt and near-despair, the amazing fact is that she eventually emerged with a deep confidence in God and faith that He would see her through any trouble.

She is now a skilful mouth artist. She signs her pictures Joni PTL – it stands for Praise the Lord.

His grace is sufficient unto me.

2 Corinthians 12: 9

Magnificent blooms by the River Ness, Inverness

Country garden beauty at Great Dixter, Northiam, East Sussex

Change and Growth

Change for better
or for worse,
At the time, for worse,
May be better
In the long run.

Deb Smith

Glad that I live am I,
That the sky is blue;
Glad for the country
lanes
And the fall of dew

After the sun the rain,
After the rain the sun;
This is the way of life,
Till the work be done

All that we need to do,
Be we low or high,
Is to see that we grow
Nearer the sky.

Lizette Woodworth Reese

Sutton Courtenay Village, Oxfordshire

Mature Faith

The Old Testament Book of Job is full of wonderful poetry about the natural world. But it is really concerned with the question, Why do people suffer?

Here is the story of a good man who suffers total disaster. He loses all his children and property and is afflicted with leprosy. His friends suggest a logical reason for what has happened: since God rewards good and evil, Job's suffering must mean that he has sinned. Job is not convinced by their arguments. He feels great bitterness and anger because he is sure God is not punishing him for wrong-doing.

Finally he comes to the conclusion that only God has the answer, only God is all-wise and the created world is proof enough of His greatness and wisdom. Job's response is humility and worship:

> *I talked about things I did not understand,*
> *about marvels too great for me to know . . .*
> *In the past I knew only what others had told me,*
> *but now I have seen you with my own eyes.*
>
> Job 42:3, 5

The bridge at Bakewell, Derbyshire

A regal rose – Coronation Gold – in full-blown glory

'. . . the flight of birds and the patterns of passing clouds.'

Patience

Patience wasn't her real name, but it would have suited her well. Physically she had suffered a great deal; old age and constant pain took their toll on her mobility and manual skills. She came to terms with her limitations and dependence on others only after fierce inner conflict.

But as she won through, her acceptance was more positive than mere resignation. After her operations for cataracts she took up reading again more avidly than before, so grateful for the large-print books. She delighted in the flight of birds and the patterns of passing clouds.

The same positive acceptance showed in her dealings with people. She recognised our weaknesses and faults, but always looked for the good in us.

The secret of her patience was in her faith. She knew that when the time was right she would have done with her frail old body and would enter into a fuller, richer, closer relationship with the one she had been following. Meanwhile, she had every confidence that

. . . nothing can separate us from his love

Romans 8:38

Hands

During the War in a bombed-out German church, a life-size statue of Jesus survived intact except for the hands which were destroyed.

Later, a sculptor offered to carve new hands for it, but the members of the church decided they would rather leave it damaged, 'Because, you see, the statue reminds us that Christ has no hands on earth but ours to do his work.'

> *Christ has no body now on earth but yours,*
> *no hands but yours, no feet but yours. . .*

When I'm ill, or disabled, or getting old, these familiar words of Saint Teresa might not seem to apply to me. In fact, it's easy to feel I'm no use to anyone.

Well, maybe my hands and feet don't function too well these days, but I can still be of use to people in more subtle ways.

The attention I give when someone speaks, the way I look when they're bustling around me, my appreciation when they do things for me . . . all can help to make or mar their day.

Coventry Cathedral

Illustration of mystic and author Julian of Norwich by Tim Hunt

Reaching Out

Jesus said to the paralysed man, 'Stretch out your hand.' He stretched it out and became well again.

Jesus, and later, some of His disciples, often stretched out a hand to heal someone.

There are times when I feel too low even to try to pray. No words will come. It is enough just to hold my hands with the palms upwards, asking for help.

There are times, too, when someone I meet is in need of the life-giving touch. My outstretched hand may be a special gift of love and understanding, or just recognition, of that person at that moment.

View of Dunfermline Abbey, Fife

In My Small Corner

Lord, make me an instrument of Thy peace.
Where there is hatred, let me sow love.
Where there is injury, pardon.
Where there is doubt, faith.
Where there is despair, hope.
Where there is darkness, light,
and where there is sadness, joy.

O Divine Master, grant that
I may not so much seek to be consoled as to console.
To be understood as to understand.
To be loved, as to love.
For it is in giving that we receive.
It is in pardoning that we are pardoned.
And it is in dying that we are born to eternal life.

Attributed to St. Francis of Assisi

Aster 'Audrey' *(novi belgii)*

Few sights can match an English country garden in full bloom

The Cross

How often have we heard the words, 'What have I done to deserve this?' The fact is, we cannot avoid suffering. There is light and darkness, good and evil, life and death, and that's the kind of world we live in.

And Jesus gets hurt too. He comes into our human life and shares our pain.

He knows bereavement:
  He grieved with
  Martha and Mary.
He knows loneliness,
  feeling cut off from
  God.
He knows the pain of
  body and limbs,
  hunger and thirst.
He knows the
  disappointment
  of thwarted plans
  and dashed hopes.
He came into the world
  and His love was
  rejected. He was
  crucified.

A bare wooden cross emphasises
the brutal reality of the crucifixion

Resurrection

But the empty tomb shows that Love is not dead.
Christ is risen. His Love is far greater than human hatred and
has won the victory for ever.
His Good News is light out of darkness
　　　　　　　good out of evil
　　　　　　　life out of death.
How do I work this out in my own experience?
　Can I look for a pearl of great beauty in the wounded
oyster shell?
　Can I see wings emerging from the shrivelled crysalis?

Small tortoiseshell butterfly on asters

Wonder

Lord Jesus, when pain rises over the horizon
And threatens to engulf me
I recoil in terror
So I stand awe-struck as I watch you choose
Not life, but death
Not glory, but grief
Not joy, but sorrow
Not a crown, but a cross
And I marvel
For mine were the sufferings you carried
You were pierced through for my faults
Crushed for my sins
On you was being laid
A punishment that brings me peace
Because of your wounds
I enjoy healing
Such knowledge is too vast for me to grasp
But as I take it in
I worship you in wonder, love and praise.

Joyce Huggett

Lulworth Cove, Dorset

Chipping Campden, Gloucestershire

Freedom

A film producer kept chained in an underground cell by Mafia kidnappers for nearly eighteen months wrote of the impact the ordinary world had on him upon his release.

'After the first few days of shock and noise, dazzling sunlight, human voices, the train ride home, embracing my wife and family, I see everything about me with new significance. Colours are more intense. The greenness of leaves, always present, is stupendous now.

The faces of a wife and sons are now joys thrilling beyond description. I gaze at these faces and listen to voices I hear. I am constantly hugging everybody.

One experiences the goodness of food well-cooked and served, kindness and care and clean clothes as though for the first time. It is all too much. It happens so suddenly.

And yet I feel these realities will never fade again for me. I feel a new peace. Love and hate are now for me clearly defined. I can only hate the evil I know and cherish the love it makes me see.'

Lord, how manifold are Thy works!
I will praise Thee with my whole heart.

Psalm 104: 24

Eyes to see

An artist sitting on the Sussex Downs was so moved by the beauty of the scenery that he wanted to sketch it. He had no pencil or drawing pad with him, only the brown paper bag his sandwiches were in.

'If only I had some chalk,' he muttered to himself.

He didn't realise that all the time he was surrounded by acres of it! The South Downs are part of a chalk ridge that stretches for miles.

Open my mind's eye to the good
In all that surrounds me.
In the joy of loving and being loved.
In the beauty of the world.
In the homeliness and comfort of familiar things.
In the changing seasons and the rhythm of life.
In the happy face of a little child
And in the wrinkles of one who has suffered.

Lift up the stone and you will find me,
Cleave the wood and I am there.

West Dean, Sussex

The coastline at Eastbourne, Sussex

Brockhampton, Gloucestershire

Quality of Life

It does not matter how shut in we are. Dawn, seen through a sick woman's window, however narrow, pulses with the same fresh wonder as it does over the whole width of the sea. One violet is as sweet as an acre of them. And it often happens – as if by a kindly law of compensation – that those who have only one violet find the way through its narrow, purple gate into the land of God, while many who walk over carpets of them do not so much as know that there is a land or a way.

Mary Webb

A parish priest visiting an elderly lady in hospital:

'What sort of a night did you have?'

'It was rather noisy, the patient in the next bed couldn't settle, poor dear, she had a terrible cough. But it meant I was able to watch the dawn.'

Dunderave Castle, Loch Fyne

Memory

Think of the rock from which you were hewn,
the quarry from which you were dug.

Isaiah 51:1

Looking back need not become an obsession, but it can be a valuable exercise. I would never have become the person I am without my past. Recalling occasions and people who have touched my life, retreading the way I have come, can teach me about the present and the future. I might find some bitterness and resentment lurking deep inside that needs to be brought out into the open. I most certainly shall find cause for humility and thankfulness and confidence to face today and tomorrow.

Laurens van der Post in his novel *A Far-off Place* puts it like this:

> *Until one acknowledges one's whole past, however*
> *painful and humiliating the process might be, and*
> *dignifies it with an honest, frank and full admission*
> *of its nature, into one's daylight self, one is not free*
> *for a future of one's own.*

The Brimham Rocks, near Pateley, Yorkshire

Confidence

Faith

What is faith? It is a way of knowing.
It is an attitude of trust.
It has to do with confidence.

True faith is not just saying, 'I believe in God'. It is actually trusting my whole life to Him and knowing He is with me whatever happens.

A bridge was built over a motorway. It was assumed to be safe. Infinite care had gone into its construction, from the draughtsman's designs, through the testing of materials, to the final completion.

'I declare this bridge open', pronounced the VIP.

'We believe it will serve many generations', declared the engineers.

'I'll be the first to ride my motor bike over it', said a youngster. He had faith!

You are my refuge and my stronghold,
my God in whom I put my trust.

Psalm 91:2

Looking through Forth Road Bridge at sunset

Pistyll Rhaiadr, North Wales

Experience

I waited patiently for the Lord
and he inclined to me and heard my cry.

He brought me up from the pit of roaring waters
out of the mire and clay
and set my feet upon a rock
and made firm my foothold.

O Lord, my God,
great are the wonderful things which you have done,
and your thoughts which are towards us:
there is none to be compared with you.

As for me, I am poor and needy:
but the Lord will care for me.

Psalm 40:1–2, 6, 21

Dove Dale, Derbyshire

God knows me personally

Even the hairs of your head have all been counted.
Matthew 10:30

We sometimes find difficulty in believing that God is love when faced with the suffering in the world and the trials and tribulations of our personal lives.

The Gospel does not say that when a hair falls from our heads it is because God allows it or causes it. He notices the loss. He gives us the grace to accept this loss; to rise above it in such a way that, incredible as it may seem, we may be happier bald than with hair!

God does not send disaster upon us nor does He protect us against disaster. He inspires us to love, to struggle and to hope in the midst of disaster.

Louis Evely

Inveraray Castle, Strathclyde

Mill on Shalford Water, Surrey

Early Autumn in Epping Forest, Essex

Into the Unknown

I said to the man who stood
  at the gate of the year,
'Give me a light that I may tread
  into the unknown.'
And he replied,
'Go out into the darkness
  and put your hand
  into the hand of God.
That shall be to you
  better than light
  and safer than a known way.'
So I went forth
  and finding the hand of God,
  trod gladly into the night.
And he led me towards the hills
  and the breaking of day
  in the lone East.

Minnie Louise Haskins

Landscape near St Just in Roseland, Cornwall

Ending or Beginning?

I have seen death too often to believe in death.
It is not an ending – but a withdrawal.
As one who finishes a long journey,
  Stills the motor,
  Turns off the lights,
  Steps from his car
And walks up the path
To the home that awaits him.

        Blanding

Peace I leave with you, my peace I give unto you.
Let not your heart be troubled, neither let it be afraid.

        John 14:27

The rose Baby Masquerade

House at Claverley, Salop

Faithful friends old . . .

Beyond Death

A patient felt that death was not far off and asked her doctor to give her some reassurance about the after-life. For a time the doctor just held her hand, not finding the right words.

Then there was a scratching at the door. The doctor's dog had jumped out of the car window, found its master's scent and followed it into the house. The doctor let the dog into the room and found what the patient needed to hear: the dog had never been there before, it just knew that its master was there and that was enough: it wanted to be with him.

Our road will take us through unknown passages to a door we can't open ourselves; but if we know that Jesus is on the other side of it and will open it for us, all shall be well.

> *All shall be well,*
> *And all shall be well,*
> *And all manner of things shall be well.*
> *Julian of Norwich*

. . . and young

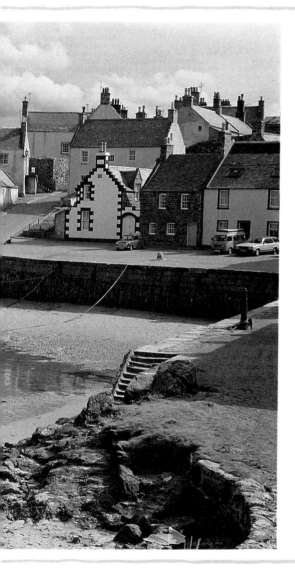

Peace

Lead me from Death to Life,
  From Falsehood to Truth.

Lead me from Despair to Hope,
  from Fear to Trust.

Lead me from Hate to Love,
  from War to Peace.

Let Peace fill our hearts,
  our world, our universe.

Love

O Love that wilt not let me go,
I rest my weary soul in Thee:
I give Thee back the life I owe,
That in Thine ocean depths its flow
May richer, fuller be.

George Matheson

Houses and harbour, Portsoy, Grampian

A Very Present Help

Lord of all hopefulness, Lord of all joy,
Whose trust ever child-like no cares could destroy,
Be there at our waking and give us, we pray,
Your bliss in our hearts, Lord, at the break of the day.

Lord of all kindliness, Lord of all grace,
Your hands swift to welcome, your arms to embrace,
Be there at our homing and give us, we pray,
Your love in our hearts, Lord, at the eve of the day.

Lord of all gentleness, Lord of all calm,
Whose voice is contentment, whose presence is balm,
Be there at our sleeping and give us, we pray,
Your peace in our hearts, Lord, at the end of the day.

Jan Struther

St. Ives, Cornwall

Muirtown Locks, Inverness

Time and Seasons

To everything there is a season
*   and a time to every purpose under the heaven.*
a time to be born and a time to die;
*   a time to plant and a time to uproot;*
a time to kill and a time to heal;
*   a time to pull down and a time to build up;*
a time to weep and a time to laugh;
*   a time for mourning and a time for dancing;*
a time to scatter stones and a time to gather them;
*   a time to embrace and a time to refrain from embracing;*
a time to seek and a time to lose;
*   a time to keep and a time to throw away;*
a time to tear and a time to mend;
*   a time for silence and a time for speech;*
a time to love and a time to hate;
*   a time for war and a time for peace.*

Ecclesiastes 3:1–8

Askrigg Church and deep snow in Wensleydale, North Yorkshire

Today

Look to this day!
For it is life, the very life of life.
In its course
lie all the virtues and realities of your existence:
the bliss of growth,
the glory of action,
the splendour of achievement.
For yesterday is but a dream,
tomorrow is only a vision,
but today well-lived makes yesterday a dream of happiness
and every tomorrow a vision of hope.
Look well therefore to this day!
Such is the salutation to the dawn.

3rd Century Indian

Remember that today is the very first day
of the rest of your life.

Cotswold village charm at Lower Slaughter, Gloucestershire

ISBN 0-7117-0416-3 © Copyright Jarrold Colour Publications 1989.
Designed and Produced by Parke Sutton Limited, Norwich for
Jarrold Colour Publications, Norwich.
Origination by Blackfriar's Colour Repro. Norwich. Printed in Portugal.